THE WEEKEND CRAFTER

Painting Glass

THE WEEKEND CRAFTER

Painting Glass

Stylish designs and practical projects

MOIRA NEAL

AND LYNDA HOWARTH

Lark
Books

First published in the USA by
Lark Books, 50 College St., Asheville, NC 28801

For information about distribution in the U.S., Canada the U.K.,
Europe, and Asia, call Lark Books at 828-253-0467.

Distributed in Australia by Capricorn Link (Australia) Pty Ltd., P.O. Box 6651,
Baulkham Hills Business Centre, NSW 2153, Australia

Distributed in New Zealand by Southern Publishers Group, 22 Burleigh St., Grafton,
Auckland, NZ

Library of Congress Cataloging-in-Publication Data
Neal, Moira.
    Painting glass : stylish designs and practical projects to paint in a weekend /
Moira Neal, Lynda Howarth.
        p. cm. — (The weekend crafter)
    Reprint. Originally published under title: Painting glass in a weekend.
London : New Holland, 1997.
    Includes index.
    ISBN 1-57990-029-1 (pbk.)
    1. Glass craft. 2. Glass craft—Patterns. 3. Glass painting and staining.
4. Glass painting and staining—Patterns. I. Howarth, Lynda. II. Title. III. Series.
TT298.N43 1998
748.5—dc21   97-28543
                                                               CIP

10 9 8 7 6

Originally published in the United Kingdom in 1997 by New Holland (Publishers) Ltd.

Copyright © 1997 New Holland (Publishers) Ltd. All rights reserved.

Editor: **Gillian Haslam**
Designer: **Peter Crump**
Photographer: **Shona Wood**
Editorial Direction: **Yvonne McFarlane**

Printed in Malaysia

All rights reserved

ISBN 1-57990-029-1

To Tony and Jim

CONTENTS

INTRODUCTION 6

GETTING STARTED 8

PROJECTS AND GALLERIES 16

Goldfish plate 18

Olive oil bottles 20

Faux tortoiseshell plate 22

Yellow gallery 24

Millefiori lantern 26

Ruby and gold sundae glasses 28

Historical gallery 30

Antiqued Etruscan-style vase 32

Fifties-style carafe and tumblers . 34

Stained glass mirror 36

Tasseled champagne glasses 38

Blue, gold, and silver gallery 40

Sunflower plate 42

Starry oil burner 44

Black, silver, and gold gallery 46

Perfume bottle 48

Decorated wine glasses 50

Frosted glass window 52

Floral roundels 54

Turquoise gallery 56

Marbled plate 58

Grapevine clip frame 60

Pasta jar 62

Textured fruit tumblers 64

Red gallery 66

Christmas platter 68

Templates 70
Acknowledgments 78
Index 79

INTRODUCTION

Decorating glassware has been a popular craft for centuries and, indeed, some of the glass in this book has been inspired by old Venetian work. Now that there are so many excellent products on the market, glass painting is enjoying an enormous revival and every craft magazine or booklet contains yet more ideas and designs.

We have inspired, supported, amused, and entertained each other for almost twenty years. On many occasions, our children have been reared in the inevitable chaos associated with combining our talents in creative ventures. We both became interested in glass-painting when a new product, Porcelaine 150, became available which has very good dishwasher resistance and is safe to use with foods — this idea really appealed and has revolutionized the craft. It means that as well as making purely decorative items or ones that need careful hand-washing, everyday glassware may be painted and will stand up to repeated dish-washing.

During the past few months we have been busy painting, stenciling, sponging, marbling, and etching any and every glass item in our homes, our friends' and parents' homes. Our craving to embellish has included anything from humble jelly jars and wine bottles to carafes and glasses, mirrors, and even window panes ... nothing has escaped the Lynda and Moira treatment. It has led to our homes being filled with glasses no-one is allowed to drink from in case they dare drop them before this book is printed!

Trips for the weekly marketing have taken on a new appeal. Never mind what the product is, tastes like, or costs — what will the bottle look like, if given a coat of paint? This has led to severe confusion. Just what IS that strange yellow stuff in that jelly jar in the refrigerator? Is it mustard dressing, lemon-and-honey vinaigrette, or custard? And how long does it keep for? If only we had labeled things before parting the mysterious contents from their beautiful containers!

And as for Jim, Lynda's husband — he became increasingly bewildered that the sponge cloth used for washing the dishes was getting smaller by the day (it was a truly marvelous discovery when we found just how good they are for sponging glassware!) All we can say is thank you Jim for putting up with us, our mess, our glass, our experiments, and our masterpieces! It has certainly spared Tony, who, as anyone who has read *Dough Craft in a Weekend* will know, has a strong aversion to Moira and her mess!

We have had enormous fun putting together all the ideas in this book and we hope that you will be inspired by them. No particular artistic skill is required as we have described, step-by-step, how to arrive at the finished designs. We have provided templates and patterns where necessary but you will see from the gallery shots just how much stylish glassware can be made with just a few simple brushstrokes and dots of outliner.

Have fun!

Moira and Lynda... partners in design

GETTING STARTED

One of the greatest advantages of painting on glass is that the craft requires very little in the way of specialized tools or equipment – just a plentiful supply of new or old glassware which can be picked up for very little money. You will probably discover that much of the equipment listed below can be found around the home. This chapter explains the different paints and demonstrates the basic decorating techniques used in the projects that follow later in the book. Once you have mastered these, you will be able to create a wide range of effects and finishes and adapt them to make your own patterns.

SOURCING GLASSWARE

If, like us, you are delighted to have an excuse to go to a flea market or yard sale, glass painting gives you the perfect reason! So much beautiful old glassware is available in an abundance of shapes and sizes at very reasonable prices. Even a batch of dissimilar glasses can be united into a set, simply by painting them with the same color or design motifs.

Look for unusual items such as goldfish bowls, old perfume bottles, engraved glasses, picture frames, clip-frames, mirrors, and vases.

Make sure you clean your glass very thoroughly before you begin painting. Really stubborn stains inside bottles may be removed with denture cleaner dissolved in hot water. Adhesive labels and decals can often be removed by rubbing with a drop of nail polish remover on a pad of absorbent cotton.

EQUIPMENT AND MATERIALS

Your local craft store, hardware store, or mail order company will be able to supply the glass paints and other basic materials to get you started. Begin with just a few colors and add to them gradually as your skill and enthusiasm grow. The other equipment you will need to begin is listed in detail in the center column of this page.

As soon as you have bought your glass paints you will be inspired to make a start. Do not be surprised if your first efforts look very amateurish as it can take a few projects to master this skill. It is therefore a good idea to start off with a really simple design on a jelly jar in order to become familiar with the texture of the paint and its application.

It will not be long before you have exhausted your own supply of plain glass and will be requesting friends and relatives to collect empty containers for you too. Everyday packaging suddenly becomes remarkably interesting once the labels are removed and a little imagination is employed!

Interesting jars, bottles, and glassware
Good quality brushes, no 2 and 4
Glass paints according to the project required. Some are solvent-based and suitable for decorative items. For more durability, choose oven-bake water-based paints
Outliner in a variety of colors
Mineral spirits
Jelly jar
Kitchen paper towels
Low-tack masking tape
Pencil
Scalpel with no 11 blade or craft knife
Tracing paper
Cocktail sticks (toothpicks)
Sponge or fur fabric
Cotton swabs
Cellophane
Hairdryer
Apron
Newspaper, to protect your worksurface
Additional useful items for styling your finished work include raffia and florist's wire

TIP

To keep the mess to a minimum, once you are ready to begin, protect your workspace with layers of old newspaper or an old tablecloth as some of the paints are solvent-based and may damage some surfaces.

If children are going help with the painting, make sure they are also well covered up.

SAFETY NOTES

There is no reason why children cannot enjoy the hobby of glass painting as well as adults. Make sure that they are supervized at all times and choose water-based paints for them to use. Store paints and brush cleaner in a cool place, well out of the reach of prying hands, when not in use.

Always follow manufacturers' specific instructions regarding the baking process if it is required (see facing page for more details).

A collection of glassware ready for painting

mainly transparent and quick drying. Replace the tops to prevent evaporation. Brushes need to be cleaned using a compatible solvent, generally mineral spirits. These paints are flammable and should not be used near a naked flame nor should children use them unsupervised. Make sure your work area is well ventilated.

SAFETY NOTE

Please refer to manufacturer's specific user and safety instructions regarding all glass paints. As a general rule, never paint any surface which is to come into contact with food unless the paint is non-toxic (this is why we decorated the backs of the plates) and as an extra pre-caution, avoid the lip line on glasses which are going to be functional and not simply used as decorations.

GLASS PAINTING PRODUCTS

Many types of paint for painting on glass are available on the market . They tend to fall into several categories:

1 Water-based paints. These do not need baking and are ideal for items which will not require washing. These are also best for children to use.

2 Water-based paints. These need to be oven-baked at 400 degrees for 30 minutes. Items painted with these colors are hand-washable. The colors are bright and dense, and easy to apply.

3 Porcelaine 150, Pébéo's water-based paints. These are baked at 300 degrees. They are completely safe when in contact with food and have good dishwasher resistance. They are ideal paints for tableware and glasses and we have used them extensively in this book. They are available in a huge range of colors, both transparent

and opaque, and once baked feel wonderfully smooth. Practice may be needed with them, as indeed with all paints, to achieve the density of cover required. It is often better to sponge on two light coats, allowing the first to dry before applying the second. There is a matt medium in the range which, if used alone, gives a wonderful, frosted effect. Used with the other colors in the range as instructed, it gives a matt finish without affecting the color.

4 Pébéo's water-based gel paints. There is a new water-based gel on the market which allows three-dimensional color to be applied to glassware direct from the tube or with the aid of a palette knife. Glass nuggets, tiny mirrors, and other items may then be embedded in the gel before it sets, to achieve an exotic effect. This enables you to imitate various blown glass effects, as well as creating stylish jewelry. The gel is available in a range of colors, and liquifies when shaken or stirred so it may also be applied with a brush.

5 Solvent-based paints. These tend to be the paints associated with the traditional, stained-glass look and are

OUTLINING

The outliners used in this book are water-based, although there are some which become permanent with baking. They can be difficult to control, so practise on jelly jars or cellophane, before embarking on the real thing.

Have a sheet of kitchen paper ready to catch any blobs of outliner from the tube which may appear as soon as the top is removed. Start by making a row of dots and you will soon realise how little pressure is required on the tube. Progress to circles, squares, triangles, and lines ①, using the practice templates on page 76. You may find you get a halo effect at times — don't worry

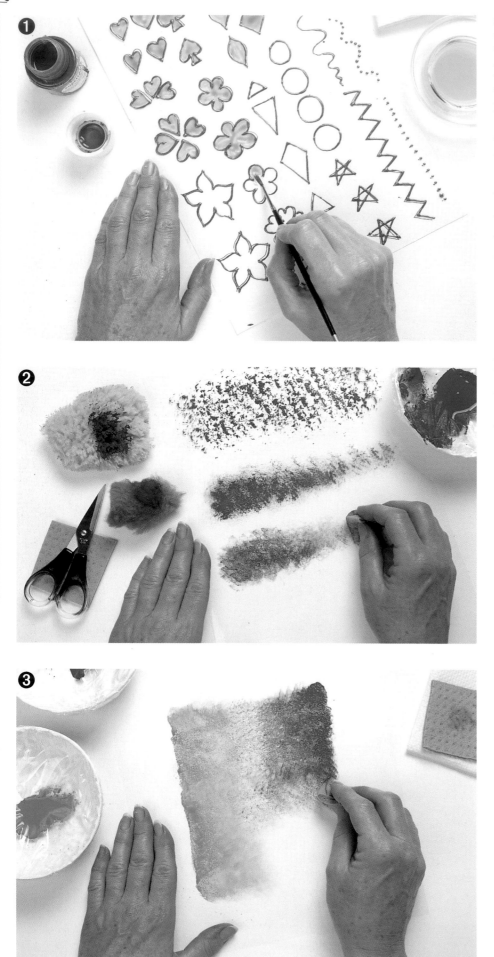

as this can be salvaged, because once the outliner has dried it can be eased back into place with the scalpel. A hairdryer is useful for speeding up the drying times of both outliners and paints but needs to be kept at least 6 inches away from the surface to avoid damage.

USING THE GLASS PAINTS

Within about five minutes, the outliner will be dry enough to apply the paint. A soft brush is essential for smooth application of the paints ①. Try filling in some of the shapes you have made with the outliners. Apply the paint with even strokes. Keep a cotton swab nearby to correct any errors and a small jar of water, mineral spirits, or solvent for brush-cleaning.

SPONGING

Sponging gives a soft, delicate effect and is a very quick and easy way to apply glass paints.

Tip a few drops of the paint into a saucer (covered with plastic wrap to reduce the cleaning up.) Gently dip your sponge pad in the paint and wipe any excess off against the edge of the dish, and then test the effect on a piece of cellophane or an old jelly jar before starting your project.

One color can be used on its own to produce a graded effect just by applying more paint onto the lowest part of the item, reducing the pressure and contact as you move up ②. A graduated effect is achieved by using several colors in

---

TIP

Thin sponge dishcloths are ideal for glass painting as they can be cut up into small pieces and discarded after use. Fine fur fabric also produces an even sponged finish but the rough edges should be folded in before use to prevent any fibers migrating onto the surface of the glass.

SPONGE DOT APPLICATORS

succession, allowing each one to merge into the next ③.

A really simple way to apply uniform dots to a project is to make your own applicators. Peel a kitchen sponge into two and then cut it into ¾-inch squares. Bind each one over the end of a cocktail stick or toothpick, using fuse wire. Make several, as you will find them a useful addition to your equipment kit!

STENCILLING

This is a good way to decorate glassware with a regular repeat pattern. It is particularly useful if you intend to sell your finished items, as it can be done very quickly, once the initial stencil-cutting is complete.

To make your stencils, photocopy the required template (see page 77), use adhesive mount to attach it to the card you are using, and allow the glue to dry for about ten minutes before attempting to cut it. Protect your worksurface with a cutting mat, cork mat, or a thick layer of newspaper before you start. Use a metal ruler as a guide for cutting straight lines ①. Avoid trying to cut around angular designs in one go; instead, make several shorter cuts ②.

It is worth taking care in order to get good, professional results and the initial investment in a craft knife or scalpel and plenty of spare blades is worthwhile. For one-off stencils to decorate flat surfaces, thin card is ideal or even a good quality paper. If you are using your stencil on a curved surface, you may need to use either thin paper or specialist adhesive stenciling film which molds more easily to the contours of the glass.

USING STENCILS

Lightly spray the back of the stencil with aerosol glue and press it onto the object to be decorated. On cylindrical items you may also need to secure the stencil with a couple of rubber bands.

hearts, flowers, initials, ring reinforcements or indeed any shape you care to cut out of paper.

Use aerosol adhesive mount to apply your own shapes to the glass. Masking tape, torn strips of newspaper, and very thin tape available from art stores can also be used. Squares, oblongs, stripes of varying widths, and harlequin designs are all possible this way, producing very effective results ①, ②.

It is easy to produce beautiful glassware with minimal artistic ability, using these ideas. The masked-off area can later be embellished with outliner to add a relief pattern, such as the veining on a leaf. This method can also be used to add a regular pattern, for example to the outer edge of a plate.

Simple, Shaker-style stencil, ideal for beginners

③ Pour a little glass paint into a saucer and use either a piece of old sponge or fur fabric to apply the paint. It is always worth experimenting at this stage. We found that fur fabric works wonderfully well for a fine, even texture. Sponge will give a rougher, less even texture which is more suitable for country-style projects ④.

MASKING AND REVERSE STENCILLING

Many different objects can be used to mask out clear areas on the glass before you decorate with sponging or marbling. Stick on shapes like stars,

ETCHING

This is a very good way to add decoration without having to use another color. It is perfect for adding details like feathers, scales on fish, eyes, and so on, as well as creating abstract designs on a sponged surface. You will need to etch the design as soon as the paint has been applied. There are several ways of doing this. Use a cocktail stick or toothpick for very fine designs or for details on tiny items. A typist's "pencil" type eraser is ideal for chunkier etching and may be sharpened with a knife or pencil sharpener depending on the effect required ①. Knitting needles work well too.

MARBLING

A wonderful range of patterns may be produced using this technique which involves floating colored solvent-based glass paints on a suitable medium. We have kept the procedure simple and have avoided the use of specialist marbling mediums in preference for water and wallpaper paste. You will need to use a bowl larger than the size of the item to be marbled and cover the worksurface with plenty of paper before you begin.

Two of the projects in this book have marbling as one of the stages of producing the final item. Refer to pages 22 and 58 for fuller instructions.

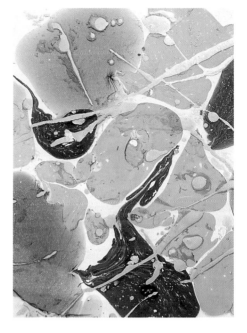

Sponged and etched snowflake plate

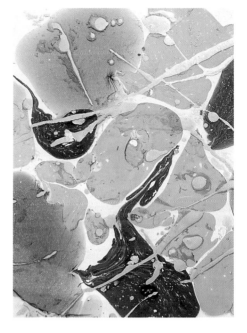

An exotic effect created by marbling a
simple piece of glass

TRANSFERRING DESIGNS

The easiest way to transfer a design onto glass is to trace it. Tape the design to the inside or back of the object to hold it firmly against the glass. If the surface is curved, make many small vertical slits to enable the pattern to shape itself to the glass. Trace over the pattern with outliner.

NARROW-NECKED BOTTLES

It is impossible to tape a design to the inside of a narrow-necked bottle but there is a simple solution. Make sure the bottle is dry inside and then, on a piece of paper, cut out the design to the height of the bottle. Roll up the paper, push it into the bottle, then pour in pasta or lentils right up to the top and the design is perfectly anchored! ①

❷

❶

EMBELLISHMENTS

The addition of those lovely shiny glass nuggets available in a myriad of colors gives a very splendid finish to an otherwise ordinary item. Tiny rhinestones and sequins may be used too and they are available from craft stores or by mail order ②.

Apply them to your glassware before the paint using a specialist glass glue to

REVERSE PAINTING TECHNIQUE

This is a very handy way to decorate the back of a glass plate so that the cutting surface will not become

damaged when the plate is used. It is also useful if you wish to use paints which are not safe when in contact with foods. A little planning is needed before you begin because the details, normally left until last, must be painted on first. Just think in reverse and remember to reverse any text too!

These iridescent nuggets inspired this floral design

Matt medium was applied over a star stencil for this subtle effect

ensure good adhesion. If you are giving a filled, decorated bottle to a friend as a gift, spend some time adding a label, a pretty stopper, or sealing wax. See our gallery pages for more ideas. Remember, a beautifully presented item will quickly lead to orders if you want to sell your glassware.

INSPIRATION FOR DESIGNS

Wrapping paper, gift cards, coloring books, curtain fabrics, flower and bulb catalogues are good sources of inspiration. Remember that you may not sell any work in which you have used other people's designs.

For a baby gift you could use the nursery wallpaper design to inspire the edge of a mirror or picture frame. Glasses, jugs, and carafes decorated to match existing china or table linen make excellent gifts for adults and may be themed to celebrate a special occasion, such as a milestone birthday or anniversary.

If you enjoy museums, why not visit one and get inspiration from old

Venetian glassware? We found some fascinating pieces in which much of the design is made up of dots and swirls — very easy to reproduce as you will see from our Historical Gallery on page 30.

This design was adapted from traditional East European glassware

PROJECTS AND GALLERIES
FOR PAINTING GLASS

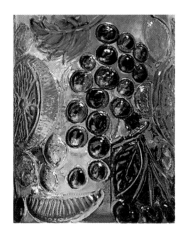

GOLDFISH PLATE

A shoal of golden fish swim around this plate which is both practical and attractive. You could use it to brighten up your bathroom, and could decorate other items such as a soap-dish or toothbrush mug to match. As the plate is decorated on the underside, it may be used for serving foods.

1 Wash the plate in hot soapy water and dry carefully. Start by sponging the edge of the plate on the underside with the gold paint, applying it densely around the outside. Allow the paint to look feathery on the inner edge. Use the paper towel and mineral spirits to clean any paint from the front of the plate.

YOU WILL NEED

A glass plate
Solvent-based glass paints in gold and white
Fine sponge or fur fabric
White spirit
Kitchen paper towels
No 2 paintbrush
Cellophane to practice on
Kitchen paper towels
Fish and surf templates (page 70)
Adhesive tape
Paper
Pen
Scissors
Cocktail stick (toothpick)
Aerosol spray mount
Saucer covered with plastic wrap

— VARIATIONS —

This plate could be painted using oven-baked paints if you want to preserve the pattern during frequent use. It seems a pity to hide it away in a cabinet when not in use, so why not store it on a plate display stand?

2 Copy the large fish template and tape it to the inside of the plate, positioning it centrally. Working on the back of the plate, paint the fish gold, but do not apply the markings at this stage.

3 Remove the template and use it as a guide to etch in the details of the scales and gills, using the cocktail stick. Keep the tip clean with the paper towel.

4 Paint the shoal of tiny goldfish next. This time have a practice run on cellophane first as it is easier to copy the tiny shapes we have given you. Use the cocktail stick to etch in the details after every third or fourth fish. For a bit of fun, paint one little fish swimming the wrong way! Allow the plate to dry for about an hour while you make the surf template for the next stage.

5 Draw around the plate onto a piece of paper. Cut out the circle and then fold it in half four times to make 16 equal sections. Open it out flat and mark ½ inch in from the edge all the way around. Trace the surf template onto each marked section. Pour some of the white paint onto the saucer, dip the sponge into it, and wipe the excess off on the edge. Sponge the surf design all around the plate. Remove the template and quickly soften the edges of the wave design by carefully sponging over it. Turn the plate over every now and then to check what it looks like from the front. Leave the plate upside down to dry for 24 hours before use.

OLIVE OIL BOTTLES

This project would make an ideal present. After painting the the olives and leaves on the glass, we filled the bottles with finest quality olive oil and attached a small pastry brush by drilling through the handle and attaching a length of wire. Choose a brush which is slightly shorter than the bottle.

1 First, wash and dry the bottle thoroughly inside and out. Trace or photocopy the template and cut it out close to the edge of the design. Tape a piece of ribbon or string to the top for easy removal from narrow-necked bottles. Push the template into the bottle. Fill the bottle with pasta to anchor the paper in place and then stopper it firmly.

YOU WILL NEED

A tall bottle (ours is 11 inches tall) with a cork stopper	Solvent-based glass paints in brown, emerald green, yellow, red, and blue
Template (page 70)	Saucer covered with plastic wrap for mixing colors
Paper	
Pen	Mineral spirits
Scissors	Cocktail stick (toothpick)
Adhesive tape	Kitchen paper towel
Ribbon or string	Wooden pastry brush (optional)
Pasta, baking beans, or similar	Drill (optional)
No 2 paintbrush	Florist's wire (optional)

VARIATIONS

This bottle would make a lovely gift for anyone to display in their kitchen. Use this idea for salad dressings too. Artistically minded people will have fun decorating bottles of flavored oil or vinegar with sprays of chili peppers or a variety of herbs.

2 Start by painting the olive branches using the brown paint darkened with a little blue if necessary. You may find it easier to rest your hand on something of similar height (we found a paper towel-roll works very well as a cushion to steady the wrist).

3 You need to mix emerald green with a little brown and yellow to achieve the leaf shade we have used. Test the color on cellophane but remember it does not have to be botanically correct! Paint in the leaves using the illustration as a guide. Use the mineral spirits to keep your brush clean and to remove errors.

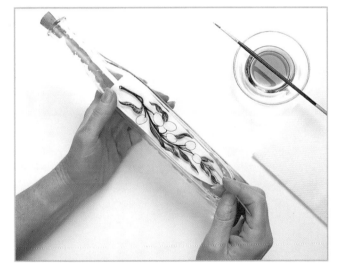

4 Etch in the details of the leaves using a cocktail stick. It is best to do this as soon as possible before the paint has time to dry. This technique really does bring the leaves to life. Alternatively, paint in the veins using a darker shade of green.

5 Finally, paint in the olives using a mixture of red, blue, and brown. If you are happy with your work, allow it to dry thoroughly. If not, remove it and start again! To give the bottle a rustic appearance, add a hook made from wire which is then twisted around the neck of the bottle. Fill the bottle with extra-virgin olive oil and then firmly wire the cork stopper in place.

FAUX TORTOISESHELL PLATE

This plate was inspired by the fascinating shapes and colors of natural tortoiseshell. Why not do as we have and create a complete set of matching glassware using different-sized bottles and pots? A combination of painting and marbling was used and we can guarantee that you will end up with a totally unique piece each time!

1 Wash and dry the plate before you begin, in order to remove any grease. Paint the back of the plate with the yellow paint, using long brushstrokes. Do not try to get this too even as imperfections will add to the natural look of the plate. Leave it to dry or speed up the process with a hairdryer.

VARIATIONS

Why stick to traditional tortoiseshell colors? As long as the base color is pale and will tone with the two marbled coats, all kinds of variations are possible. It is worth experimenting on cellophane before you reach a decision as it is much simpler to throw it out than it is to clean a plate!

2 Fill the bowl with water and then fill the eye droppers with both the brown paints. Quickly drop the paint on the surface of the water and allow the drops to merge slightly. Position the plate over the marbled effect and "roll" the plate away from you, picking up the marlbed pattern on the back of the plate (see step 4 below.)

3 For the second marbling, a more spattered effect is achieved by squirting the paints over the water so that it breaks up into smaller drops. Any unsightly blobs may be carefully removed using a cocktail stick to roll the paint off the surface of the water.

4 Again, lower the plate onto the marbled surface as indicated in step 2 above. Leave the plate upside down to dry once more. You can use a hairdryer to speed up the drying process if you wish.

5 Touch up any imperfections using a fine brush and the yellow base coat and leave to dry for at least 24 hours before use. For extra scratch resistance, the back may be painted with two coats of polyurethane varnish.

YELLOW GALLERY

"Volcano" oil burner
This has been etched and overpainted.

Tall yellow bottle
This elegant bottle has been stencil-frosted for a pretty finish.

Orange slices jar
A citrus effect was achieved by applying the paint with a very small brush and fine brushstrokes.

Shallow yellow platter
A very simple gold border was painted around this dish for a striking effect.

Cup and saucer
Luscious apricots were painted on this cup using opaque glass paints.

Shaped glasses
One glass has been painted with simple bands of yellow and gold and the other given an iridescent effect by being lightly sponged, first with gold and then with a clear yellow. A simple band of gold dots was added later.

1940s-style glass dessert dish

Bottom: The embossed lines on this dish made it very simple to decorate with yellows, orange, and gold.

Perfume bottle

Matt medium was used on this little bottle first and then the yellow paint applied, making the glass appear transparent again.

Hexagonal jar

Bottom: Low-tack tape was used to mask off alternate facets before marbling with yellow, orange, and gold. Gold outliner dots were added later.

Tall, pale yellow glass

The bowl of this glass was made from pale lemon glass but a deeper color was overlaid using clear yellow paint.

Copper glass

This glass was frosted with matt medium first before a coat of copper was sponged over the bottom section.

Stripy frosted glass

Strips of paper were used to mask off areas and matt medium then sponged on to give a frosted look.

MILLEFIORI LANTERN

This lantern was inspired by the wonderful range of colors found in millefiori beads. It is surprisingly easy to reproduce the design but can only be successfully created on a flat surface. As the panels of this lantern are removable, it is ideal for decorating in this way and candlelight enhances the rich colors.

1 Clean the panels of glass using glass cleaner, being very careful of the sharp edges. (Wear the leather gloves for protection.) Lay your glass on a sheet of paper and draw around it, and then use small coins as templates as shown. If you prefer, use the template on page 71.

VARIATIONS

Faceted bottles and jelly jars may be decorated using this method. Make sure that your chosen item is kept completely level at all times until baked.

2 Lay the panel of glass over the pattern and remove the lids from all the tubes of outliners before you begin. It is best to work on just three circles at a time and vary the color combinations using an equal amount of color overall. Begin with the red. The fluid nature of the outliners make them ideal for this project.

3 Continue to add more colors in circles and dots in an effort to achieve a star or floral effect. Note how well the colors look juxtaposed to the nearest color in the rainbow, i.e. red, orange, yellow, green, and blue. This stops complementary colors (e.g., orange and blue) merging and becoming sludgy within each "bead." Aim to use all the colors on each one and do not worry if your work looks "blobby" at this stage.

4 Once you have completed three of the "beads," use the cocktail stick to start the feathering. Drag the colors in and out all the way round each one, to create a spider's web effect and encourage the colors to blend and bleed into one another.

5 Continue to work down the panel of glass toward yourself, to avoid smudging your work. The paint looks very dense and opaque at this stage until it is thoroughly dry. When you have finished the panel, set it aside and start the next one. Note how all the colors continue to bleed into each other. This will continue to happen as the panels are left to dry flat for at least the next 24 hours. Bake, following the manufacturer's instructions. Allow to cool, and then fill in the spaces with solvent-based glass paint if you wish. Leave to dry thoroughly before reassembling the lantern.

RUBY AND GOLD SUNDAE GLASSES

The inspiration for this design comes from Middle Eastern tea glasses. If you are able to find any plain glasses, the design may be adapted to suit them.

If you are feeling adventurous, why not make a complete dinner service using this design?

1 Wash the glassware in hot soapy water, rinse, and dry thoroughly. Cover your work area with paper before you begin. Use the rubber bands to mask off a parallel strip around the dish. The width may be varied depending on the size of your dish, but be sure to make them all equidistant.

YOU WILL NEED

Set of sundae glasses
Rubber bands ¼ inch wide
Solvent-based glass paints, such as Vitrail, in ruby and gold
No 2 paintbrush
Mineral spirits for brush cleaning
Kitchen paper towels
Template (page 70)
Scalpel
Cellophane for practice runs

VARIATIONS

The dishes could each be painted in a different color as long as each is strong enough to contrast with the gold. Practice first before going on to the real thing. The central band would make an attractive decoration on wine glasses too.

2 Fill the masked off area with the ruby paint, keeping the bowl clear of the work top to avoid smudging. Keep a paper towel to hand for brush-cleaning before moving on to the next step.

3 The narrow gold bands are added next, along with the wavy gold line which forms the basis for the leaf and tendril design. Have a practice run on cellophane first, using the template (see page 70) as a guide.

4 Once you are confident painting the leaf and tendril design, paint it on the bowls. If your artistic ability is not up to it, try painting little groups of three dots or simple tendrils instead.

5 Finally, work on the saucers. The leaf design is echoed around the edge in gold, followed by groups of three red dots in between.

HISTORICAL GALLERY

Spotted 1950s-style glass
Bottom: Use a fine brush to apply spots in a variety of colors.

Hexagonal jar
Bottom: Simple brushstrokes were used for the flowers and gold-and-white leaf shapes decorate the edges.

Art Deco bottle
Simple lines and clean colors inspired by the Art Deco movement.

Miniature perfume bottles
These little bottles are surprisingly inexpensive and very quickly decorated with simple brushstrokes and outliner.

Old jelly pot
The engraved design on this delightful old jelly pot has been highlighted with gold, with fuschias delicately painted around the top.

Venetian-style bottle
The simple brushstrokes on the edges of this bottle were inspired by old Venetian glassware. The lady was painted first with an opaque white and then the green and red clear paints applied on top.

Champagne glass

Bottom: Red and green were drizzled down this old-fashioned champagne glass and dots of color added too.

Heraldic goblet

This is a good example of allowing the shape of the glass dictate the style of the embellishment. Here, the design has been added in black, white, and gold.

Thistle glass

Bottom: This engraved bargain buy has been transformed with the use of color.

Recycled perfume bottle

This beautiful lady in her crinoline dress is definitely for the more artistic reader!

Hexagonal boxes

Simple Art Nouveau motifs have been applied in gold and black.

ANTIQUED ETRUSCAN-STYLE VASE

The little stoppered jug used for this project started life filled with a salad dressing which has now become one of the anonymous substances in the refrigerator! The idea can be adapted to any bottle or pitcher you can find either hiding at the back of a cabinet or on your next trip to the supermarket. Several pieces may be decorated in a similar way to make an interesting and original display.

1 Sponge the top half of the vase with the green paint, allowing it to fade around the middle. The sponging can look quite rough, as you are aiming for an aged look. Leave for a few minutes to dry between this and the next three steps.

4 Highlight the edges of the vase with the gold, including the rim and handle. The idea is to make the worn surfaces look metallic.

2 Using the blue paint, sponge from the bottom upward, and over the first coat. Allow the paint to fade out as you work upward.

3 Antique over the base of the jug with the pewter, adding light touches of the metallic color to the neck of the jug and the handle. Again, precision is unimportant as a rough look is more authentic.

5 Paint swirls of matt medium at random on the vase. The paint looks milky when it is applied but dries to a very subtle finish.

6 Echo the swirls using the pewter outliner. This dries to give an extra dimension to the vase. Leave the vase to dry for 24 hours before baking, following manufacturer's instructions.

VARIATIONS

Try making a collection of glassware using this technique. Similar glassware is readily available and very quick to decorate in this way and several pieces could be painted at the same time.

FIFTIES-STYLE CARAFE AND TUMBLERS

This really is a 20-minute project! It is wonderfully easy to do and as the shapes are so simple, they require no artistic ability – if you can write, you can reproduce them once you have mastered using the paints.

1 Copy the template on page 71 and lay the cellophane over it in order to have a practice run if you are not sufficiently confident to start straight onto the glassware. Keep a sheet of paper towel handy and use it to keep the nozzle clean before drawing each motif. Apply the paints sparingly as they will spread slightly over the next ten minutes.

YOU WILL NEED

Carafe and six tumblers
Patterns (page 71)
Cellophane to practice on
Oven-baked outliners, such as Porcelaine 150, in green, magenta, and black
Kitchen paper towels
Scalpel or craft knife
Domestic oven

— VARIATIONS —

Why not decorate the backs of glass plates and bowls to make a complete table setting?

2 Once you are ready to start work on the glasses, wash them with hot, soapy water. The black squiggles are fun to do and it is best to do these freehand, in order to get a flowing line. The black diamond design is easiest to create in two stages, working from the top to the bottom of one side and then the next.

3 Magenta sunbursts are worked from the outside inward, making up the six spokes. The second magenta design of three wavy lines is then worked on the next glass.

4 The green triangular design is worked next and then the green dot design. Finally, transfer all of the designs to the carafe, starting with the black, followed by the magenta, and then the green. The groups of three dots can be added last of all as they are small and make good "fillers."

5 Leave all the glassware to dry for 24 hours and then use the scalpel to ease any stray outliner gently into place before baking, following the manufacturer's instructions. Wash the glassware before use.

STAINED GLASS MIRROR

The color selection of red, blue, and green has made this simple mirror look quite exotic! The outline shapes could also be used as a solid design to decorate a wine bottle or jelly jars with great success. It is easy enough for children to be able to imitate as long as they are carefully supervised, and a myriad of effects can be obtained, depending on the color selection used and the size of each shape.

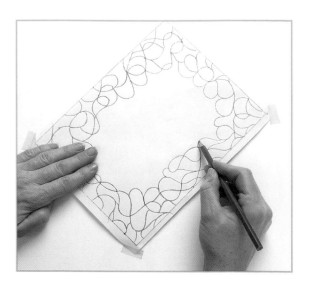

1 Use glass cleaner to remove all traces of grease from the mirror before you begin. Cut the carbon paper to the size of the mirror and lay it face down onto it. Make a copy of the template, enlarging or reducing it as required, and lay it over the carbon. Tape it in place. Use the colored pencil to copy the outline onto the mirror so that you can see what you have already traced.

YOU WILL NEED

Mirror (9 x 7 inches)
Glass cleaner
Carbon paper
Scissors
Template (page 72)
Adhesive tape
Sharp colored pencil
Paper for protecting worktop
Solvent-based paints such as Vitrail in ruby red, blue, and green
No 2 brush
Mineral spirits for brush cleaning
Hairdryer (optional)
Lead effect outliner
Kitchen paper towels
Scalpel

TIP

The beauty of this project is that precision is unimportant so don't worry too much when you are copying the outlines. You may want to have more or less of the mirror showing than we have and it is easy to adjust this in step 1 by altering the size of the template using a photocopier.

2 Now the fun begins. Load the paintbrush with red paint and allow it to flow onto the mirror. Apply the paint quite thickly to produce a rich colorful effect. Paint about one fourth of the shapes this way. Clean the brush with the mineral spirits and allow the red areas to dry before using the next color. This may be speeded up with the use of a hairdryer if you wish.

3 Apply the green to a further quarter of the shapes. It does not matter if the edges of your painted areas are uneven as the outliner will hide a multitude of sins!

4 Finally, use blue glass paint to fill in all but one fourth of the shapes. The unpainted mirrored spaces can be embellished with the addition of rhinestones, glass nuggets, or sequins, which you can secure in place with glass glue, or leave plain as we have done.

5 Now use the outliner to trace over the pencil line in the mirror. Apply even pressure to the tube and have a paper towel handy to keep the nozzle clean Finally, edge the mirror with the outliner to give a finished look. Allow the mirror to dry for about 24 hours before use, and polish off any fingerprints.

TASSELED CHAMPAGNE GLASSES

Here is an imaginative idea to transform a set of champagne glasses into unique and expensive-looking tableware. As just one color is used, there is little financial outlay and the results are stunning.

1 Wash the glasses in warm soapy water or clean them with mineral spirits. Start by cutting a piece of paper about ¾ inch wide and long enough to fit around the top of the glass and, if necessary, use a pencil to mark the cutting line. This is the template which will determine the height of the tassels but you can adjust it if you wish, provided you keep the painted design clear of the lip line of the glass.

YOU WILL NEED

Champagne flutes
Mineral spirits or warm soapy water
Paper
Pencil
Ruler
Scissors
Elastic band
Tassel and rope template (page 71)
Tube of gold Porcelaine 150 outliner
Kitchen paper towels
Domestic oven
Empty jelly jars or cellophane (optional)

TIP

Before you begin you may like to experiment with the flow of the paint by testing it on a jelly jar or cellophane first. As the paint is water-based it is easy to wipe it off and start again and again until you are proficient. It is a good idea to keep the paper towels handy to blot the nozzle before each attempt.

You will find that the paint tends to spread slightly during the following ten minutes so it is best to avoid applying it too thickly.

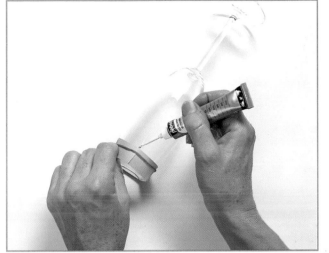

2 Fold the paper into five, open it out, and then secure it around the glass using a rubber band as shown. This is a quick and easy way to space the tassels evenly, as each fold indicates the position of a tassel.

3 Use the glass paint to make five tiny dots around the glass to mark the position of the tassels as shown. Remove the paper and repeat on each glass.

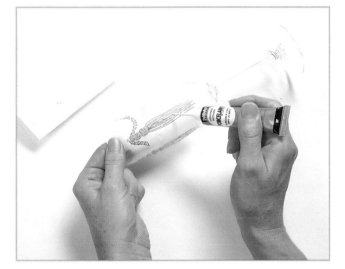

4 Cut the template to fit inside the glass and hold it in place while tracing off the tassel with the gold outliner. (Remember to clean the nozzle with a paper towel before starting each one.) Move the template around and paint all five tassels.

5 Finally, link each tassel with the rope motif. Leave in a safe place for 24 hours to dry and then bake according to the manufacturer's instructions.

—— **VARIATIONS** ——

This design is equally suited to embellish a straight-sided pitcher and matching tumblers. As the design is so quick and simple to create, it could be used to decorate a large number of glasses for a special celebration. Why not use silver outliner for a 25th wedding anniversary, for example?

BLUE, GOLD, AND SILVER GALLERY

Tiny storage jar
Below: This little jar has been decorated with a variety of shells and a starfish. It makes a great container for beads.

Heart
Bottom: These little hanging plastic hearts were decorated using silver and gold outliners.

Snowflake plate
The silver edge was sponged first, followed by the blue. A pencil eraser was used to etch the snowflake shapes.

Old-fashioned candy jar
This bottle was first sponged with white over the top part of the bottle and then, once dry, blue was sponged up from the bottom giving this wintry effect. Snowflakes were added using outliner.

Simple spiral designed glass
This delightful old glass has been brought right up to date with the simple addition of gold and blue banding.

Triangular blue bottle
Right: There is so much interestingly shaped and colored glassware on the market now which can be decorated with opaque colors.

Tiny perfume bottles
Tiny hearts and a cherub have been painted on these little bottles, using a fine brush and gold paint.

Frosted glass bottle

Bottom: This bottle started life filled with salad dressing! It was too pretty to throw away and has been transformed by being sponged with blue and silver and then decorated with silver snowflakes.

Marbled plate, bottle, and jar

Blue, white, and gold paints were floated on water and gently swirled to create these marbled patterns.

Storage jar

Here is a simple way to brighten up plain storage jars, using deliberately uneven brush marks based on squares.

Wheat vase

Twenty minutes is all you need to add this simple wheat design in gold.

Small storage jar

Above: Use simple flowers, spots, and scrolls to make this storage jar suitable for a bedroom or bathroom.

SUNFLOWER PLATE

This molded plate lends itself to being painted as a sunflower. If you are unable to buy a similar one, the design could be applied to the back of a plain plate if you make a simple template first by folding a circle of paper into equal segments. Draw a circle for the center of the flower and then stick the template onto the inside of the plate before you begin.

1 Lightly brush the petals and center of the design with the gold. Use it sparingly so that the other colors, to be applied later, will shine through. Set aside to dry.

YOU WILL NEED

Glass plate — ours is 10½ inches
Oven-baked paints such as Porcelaine 150 in gold, two shades of yellow, orange, black, and brown
Cellophane
No 2 brush
Water
Domestic oven

2 It is time to experiment now, while the gold paint dries. Use a piece of cellophane to work out the color density you want to achieve before working on the plate. Use delicate brush strokes.

3 Use the palest shade of yellow first and brush it evenly, following the direction of the petals. Work the second yellow over it, working about two-thirds of the way up the petals so that the outer edges are paler.

4 Use the orange to darken from the center of each petal to about halfway down, using the brush almost dry to give a light, feathery look.

5 The center of the sunflower is stippled, using a mixture of brown, black, and orange, to give the appearance of seeds. Leave the plate to dry for 24 hours before baking according to the manufacturer's instructions. It may then be used and washed frequently without damage.

STARRY OIL BURNER

These beautiful, simple glass burners are perfect for decorating with glass paints and can be painted, etched, or sponged to suit any occasion. They are available in several different shapes and sizes and are economical to use. No more dripping candle wax! Make sure you use oven-baked paints to prevent any lamp oil coming into contact with the surface and dissolving your creation.

1 Remove the wick and holder from the burner and plug the hole with adhesive putty. Wash the burner in hot, soapy water and dry thoroughly. Sponge the matt medium over the entire surface. Put some of the matt medium on the jelly jar too as it will be useful in step 5. The paint looks transparent when it is first applied but it dries quickly. When dry, apply a second coat. A hairdryer will speed up the process.

YOU WILL NEED

Round glass oil burner

Jelly jar

Re-usable adhesive putty (found in office supply stores)

Small piece of sponge

Oven-baked paints such Porcelaine 150 in pewter and matt medium

Porcelaine 150 pewter outliner

No 2 paintbrush

Water

Hairdryer (optional)

Large and small star templates (page 73)

Metal ruler

Scalpel with a no. 11 blade

Cutting mat

Pencil

Paper towels

Domestic oven

SAFETY NOTE

Always follow the manufacturer's instructions supplied with the lamp and never leave it unattended at any time, particularly if you have children or cats in the house.

2 Cut out the star templates using a metal ruler, cutting mat, and scalpel. (Refer to the techniques section.) Use the pencil to draw the star outline onto the globe, using the photograph as a guide for the spacing. Keep the motifs equidistant.

3 Paint the marked stars using the pewter paint. The matt base coat is a wonderful surface to paint over. For a really good cover, a second coat is needed.

4 Use the outliner to make rows of tiny dots around each star. Be careful to use the outliner sparingly as it continues to spread. Allow the globe to dry thoroughly before moving on to the next step.

5 The tiny stars are etched out using the scalpel and the template pattern provided. It is a good idea to practise on the jelly jar first, before starting on the real thing. Leave the globe to dry for 24 hours before baking, following manufacturer's instructions. Once the globe is completely cool, fill it with lamp oil, using a tiny funnel to avoid any falling onto the matt surface. Replace the wick in the bottle, and light it.

VARIATIONS

Use different colored lamp oils to make the burner look festive or spring-like. It makes a great table decoration surrounded with evergreens, but make sure leaves are kept well away from the flame.

BLACK, SILVER, AND GOLD GALLERY

Etched cork-stoppered jar
Bottom: This jar was frosted with matt medium with the design etched out afterward.

Oak and acorn glass
Bottom: This design was stencilled on and the detail etched out with a cocktail stick.

Pitcher
Bottom: As simple as ABC! Letters were drawn on the pitcher and black dots added around the top.

Black plate
These stunning white brushstrokes look very oriental but are, in fact, simple random strokes.

Cocktail glass
Two coats of gold on the outside of this glass were followed by random black spots for a stylish finish.

Marbled plate
Here black, white, and gold paints were floated on water and the design picked up on the back of the plate.

Frosted carafe
Oak leaves have been stenciled on this carafe using matt medium.

Art Deco jar

Bottom: This jar has been decorated very simply with stylised deer.

Glasses

Below: It is so easy to unite several dissimilar glasses like these by creating a matching color scheme. Black, gold, and white paints and outliners were used to apply the designs.

Christmas bauble

Not even the humble bauble can escape decoration! This one was patterned with outliner.

Art Deco perfume bottle

Center: This bottle was sponged with silver and gold before the stylised design was added in black.

Black and white dappled plate

Blobs of black and white paint were dropped onto the back of the plate and then spread and etched with a cocktail stick.

Perfume bottle

Bottom: This bottle, embellished with trefoils, was decorated in the same way as the project on page 48.

Gold and black glass

This glass was made in the same way as the set of decorated glasses with bands on page 28.

47

PERFUME BOTTLE

Have you ever thought what a pity it is to throw out your empty perfume bottles, especially when they are often such lovely shapes? Here is the answer. The design can be applied to any size or shape of bottle and a group of dissimilar bottles can be united in this way to make an attractive collection for the bedroom or bathroom.

1 Wash and dry the bottle thoroughly before you begin. Cover the entire surface by sponging it with the pewter paint. Apply two or three light coats, allowing the paint to dry between coats. In this way you will build up a really deep, lustrous surface. Allow to dry for 24 hours and bake, following manufacturer's instructions. This will make a much better surface to work on and mistakes can be easily removed.

YOU WILL NEED

Small decorative bottle or empty perfume bottle

Oven-baked glass paints such as Porcelaine 150 in pewter, black, and ivory

Fine sponge

Trefoil pattern (page 72)

Cellophane for practice runs

No 2 paintbrush

Water

Kitchen paper towels

Domestic oven

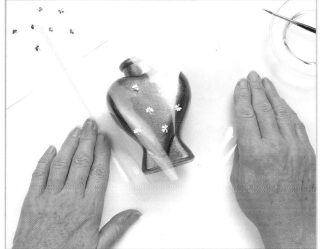

2 It is a good idea at this stage to have a practice run at painting the trefoils. To copy the pattern, lay cellophane over the template and paint as many as you need, using one color until you feel sufficiently confident to paint them freehand.

3 Check the spacing of the trefoils by laying the cellophane over your chosen bottle. This will give you an idea of how and where to place the shapes.

4 Now you are ready to start on the bottle. Paint all the ivory shapes in first, remembering to leave room for the other two colors.

5 Paint the black trefoils next and then fill in the gaps with a silvery mix of black and pewter. Leave to dry for a further 24 hours and bake again.

DECORATED WINE GLASSES

Here is a really neat way to decorate glasses and a matching carafe, with the help of just a few rubber bands. Use this technique to mask off sections, then sponge them in a single color. Neat rows of dots add a finishing touch. It's the perfect project for someone who can't draw!

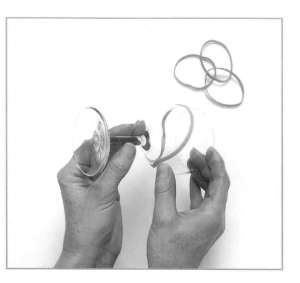

1 Wash all the items in hot soapy water and dry thoroughly. Place a rubber band around the glass ½ inch from the top on one side to the same distance from the stem at the bottom. Take time to adjust the band evenly for best results. The width of the band will determine the space between the colored areas; the band measurement given is the minimum you should use. It is advisable to avoid the lip line if using a paint other than that specified.

VARIATIONS

Add a matching carafe to the set, using a different color in each section to unite it with the glasses. Experiment with different color combinations and outliners. This idea can be adapted to make little candle-holders decorated with solvent-based paints to give a stained glass effect.

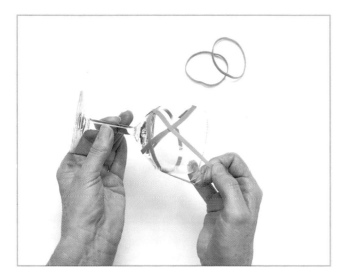

2 Repeat with the second and third rubber bands, aiming to spread them equally around the bowl of the glass so that all the sections to be painted are roughly the same size. If you are planning to decorate a carafe to match the set, add bands to it as well.

3 Pour a little paint into the saucer and then sponge the spaces between the bands with your chosen color. Apply the color lightly and evenly for best results. We painted all six areas the same color on each glass but you could use six different colors. Paint the stems too, as we have, or leave them plain. Leave for 24 hours to dry before being tempted to go on to step 4!

4 Remove the bands and you will find that the paint has seeped under the rubber band where they cross. Use a scalpel to neaten up the edges.

5 Using the outliner, apply tiny dots around each block of color, to give a really clean finish. Remember that the outliner tends to spread slightly so leave a space between each dot. (It might be worth practising first on a jelly jar.) If you are happy with the result, leave for a further 24 hours before baking, following manufacturer's instructions. If not, wash the design off and start again! Wash the glasses before use.

FROSTED GLASS WINDOW

Here is an inexpensive but attractive alternative to frosted glass. It is also a good substitute for net curtaining at windows where you need a little extra privacy. The painting may be done on the inside of an existing window if self-curing paint is used, or on a sheet of glass cut to size as we have done, in which case oven-baked paints may be used for scratch resistance. Use a photocopier to enlarge or reduce the pattern to suit any size.

1 Enlarge the pattern, using a photocopier, to the size required, if necessary. Use aerosol mount to attach it to the thin card (if using.) Leave to dry for at least ten minutes before cutting the stencil. Place the pattern onto the cutting mat and use the scalpel to cut out the design carefully. Keep the rooster for step 3.

VARIATIONS

If you omit the rooster, this design would look good as a frame for a mirror. With the addition of a few more squares, the pattern can easily be elongated and a row of roosters added!

2 Thoroughly clean the glass with warm soapy water or glass cleaner and make sure it is completely dry before sponging. Lay the glass onto a piece of colored paper or fabric so that you can see what you are doing. Use a light spray of adhesive mount on the back of the stencil, leave to dry for a few seconds, then position it centrally on the glass.

3 Pour some opaque white paint into the saucer and use the sponge or fur fabric to apply the paint evenly over the outer design. Hold the glass up to the light to check for even density. Sponge the rooster last. Remove the stencil with great care and admire before quickly moving on to the next stage!

4 Use the eraser or cocktail stick to etch in the eye, wing and other details of the rooster using the template as a guide.

5 Finally, remove any stray paint which has managed to work its way under the stencil, using a cotton swab, and then leave to dry for at least 24 hours. Alternatively, use a scalpel to remove the paint once it is completely dry. Bake if appropriate.

─── TIP ───

If using oven-baked paints, remember to use a
pane of glass which will fit inside the oven.

FLORAL ROUNDELS

These roundels make a refreshing change from the usual stained glass versions that are now seen everywhere. They are a perfect way to brighten up a window and look attractive when the sunlight shines through them.

1 If your roundel is not the same size as ours, use a photocopier to enlarge or reduce the template to the required dimmensions. Lay the template on the worksurface and tape the roundel over it, being careful to position the tape over plain areas of the pattern.

VARIATIONS

These designs could be used as jelly jar covers if the designs were worked on cellophane using black paint instead of outliner. Enlarge or reduce the design according to the size of the jar and use white tissue paper underneath to show off the design.

2 Use the outliner to carefully follow the outlines of the flowers and leaves, using steady, even pressure. Start at the top and work toward you to avoid smudging. Keep a paper towel handy to remove any blobs of outliner from the tip of the nozzle. Leave to dry or speed up the process with the hairdryer.

3 If there are any imperfections in the outlining, they can be salvaged at this stage. Use a scalpel to scratch off any rough areas and use the paintbrush to gently brush loosened outliner away from the surface.

4 Practice your brushstrokes on cellophane, using the ruby paint. Once you are confident, start working on the flowers and brush the petals from the center outward to obtain light, feathery strokes.

5 Finally, paint the leaves with the green paint, varying the density of the paint for a more realistic effect and to build up depth.

TURQUOISE GALLERY

Stoppered bottle

White lilies have been painted on this bottle, using silver for the stamens. Look through flower catalogs for similar ideas.

Tall turquoise vase

Gold outliner has been applied to give a "punched" look in simple spirals and curves.

Floral jar

Bottom: Green and silver paints were used to brighten up this jelly jar. A little white was added to the silver for the outer parts of the petals and the white dots of paint applied last.

Goldfish jar

Below: This would be fun to fill with bubble bath as a gift for a child. The fish were painted with outliner first and then with a coat of clear yellow glass paint.

Fish platter

Gold was lightly brushed on the back of this platter and then a variety of blues, greens, and turquoises painted over it.

Two-tone glass

Bottom: Transparent oven-baked paints in green and blue were sponged onto this little glass to give a graduated effect.

Marbled plate

The edge of the plate was painted with gold and allowed to dry. Then turquoise, green, purple, and gold paints were floated on water, and the plate marbled with them.

Cup and saucer

Below: Just imagine sipping fruit tea from this cup, beautifully painted with blueberries. Why not make a set featuring a variety of fruits?

Multi-faceted pitcher

This old pitcher was picked up at a thrift store and transformed by being sponged with a range of oven-bake paints. Pewter outliner was then dotted around each color.

Tall vase

Simple brushstrokes in shades of blues, greens, and gold make this a very quick and easy project.

Turquoise tumbler

Left: The black lines were applied first and then green, white and gold paints to fill some of the spaces.

Clip frame

Black outliner was allowed to trail in wiggly lines around the frame. Once it was dry, some of the spaces were filled with green, gold and purple paints.

Encrusted bottle

Chunky glass nuggets were first glued in place on this bottle and the design worked around them. The bottle has been worked in a combination of paints and outliners.

MARBLED PLATE

Decorate the back of a glass plate with this attractive combination of techniques to produce designer tableware. You may be lucky enough to have one of these plain glass plates, so popular in the 1960s, at the back of a closet. If not, they are still to be found in department stores or even at yard sales.

1 Run the tape around the plate about ¼ inch from the edge and then use this as a guide to paint the silver rim. If you have a steady hand, you will be able to do this freehand. Leave to dry thoroughly before removing the tape.

YOU WILL NEED

Glass plate	Water or a very thin solution of wallpaper paste
Adhesive tape	
Silver solvent-based paint	Eye dropper
Paintbrush	Solvent-based paints in purple and yellow, or colors of your choice
Silver outliner	
A bowl at least 3 inches larger diameter than the plate	Mineral spirits
	Newspapers
Plastic tote bag or non-PVC plastic wrap (optional)	Cellophane for practice runs
	Kitchen paper towels

— TIPS —

Before you begin the marbling, cover the worksurface with plenty of protective paper. Line the bowl with a plastic bag, if you wish, and fill with water to within 1 inch of the top. We found that this makes the cleaning up process very easy. Be warned, however, that lining the bowl with PVC plastic wrap and some other types of plastic sheeting can prevent the colors from spreading. We learned the hard way!

Experimentation is essential.

Instead of using cellophane or paper to clean the surface of the water (see step 5,) use a jar or small bottle to pick up the paint. You might end up with a really interesting piece!

2 The fine silver detailing is added at this stage using the outliner. Once the paint has been "anchored" to the rim of the plate at one side, the tube is lifted up into the air and the paint allowed to flow backward and forward across the plate in fluid lines. Occasionally it may break, but do not worry too much – it all adds to the character of the design! Allow to dry.

3 Drop the purple paint onto the surface of the water or wallpaper paste, using an eye dropper or cocktail stick. It will spread immediately. About 5 drops will be enough. For best results, speed is of the essence now.

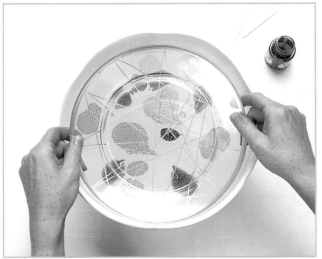

4 Using the pipette, add a few drops of the second color and then use the cocktail stick to swirl the colors gently into a pleasing pattern.

5 If you are not happy with the pattern you have created, remove it by lifting it off the surface using cellophane or paper towels and start again. When you are pleased with the result, pick up the plate at the very edges, position it over the marbled pattern and then tip it toward you slightly and down onto the marbled surface. Carefully rock the plate away from you so that it picks up the pattern on the surface of the watery solution. Turn it upside down and stand it on a small can or similar item. Use brush cleaner on a paper towel to remove any paint which has found its way onto the front of the plate, and then leave it to dry for 24 hours.

TIP

Store marbled plates with sheets of nonstick baking paper or parchment paper between them to protect the pattern. The plate can be washed, as long as it is not immersed in water which will damage the marbling. As there is no paint on the cutting surface, it is suitable for occasional use.

GRAPEVINE CLIP FRAME

This pretty clip frame couldn't be simpler! If you wish, you could substitute strawberries, cherries, or pendulous blossoms, such as wisteria or laburnum, for the grapes, depending upon your artistic ability. Use a botanical encyclopedia for inspiration.

1 Remove the glass from the clip frame and use the cleaner to thoroughly clean both sides. Lay the glass over the template and paint all the grapes with the purple paint.

— TIP —

You could use a mount to mask off an oval or oblong shape. Or how about tearing the aperture from watercolor paper, roughly following the outline of the grapes?

2 Mix the chartreuse with a little yellow and paint about half the leaves with a solid color before moving on to step 3. (Test the color first on a piece of cellophane to check you are happy with it.)

3 Once you have painted half the leaves, use the cocktail stick (toothpick) to etch in the veins. After etching each leaf, clean the point with a paper towel. If the weather is very hot, paint only a few leaves at a time before etching.

4 Pour some of the emerald paint into the saucer and then dip the sponge into it. Wipe any excess off on the edge of the saucer and then test the density of the sponging on a jelly jar or cellophane before starting on your frame. Once you have mastered the density required, work on the frame, filling in the background with the sponging.

5 Finally, use the cocktail stick once more, this time to engrave tendrils on the sponged background. Etch around the leaves too if the background is very dense behind them. Once you are pleased with the result, leave it in a safe place to dry for 24 hours before assembling it.

PASTA JAR

Brighten up your pasta jar with these colorful Italian flags. This project is perfect for a beginner as little skill is required! Tie a large bow around the jar and fill with spaghetti for an attractive, inexpensive gift.

1 Wash the pasta jar thoroughly in warm, soapy water and dry thoroughly. Cut the parchmentpaper to fit around the jar and cut off about ¼ inch down one side. Stick the paper lightly to the jar. Stick the string to the top of the jar, and then wind it around and around the jar before taping the string in place at the bottom of the jar. Aim for about three rotations. Use the string as a guide to draw a continuous line on the paper.

YOU WILL NEED

Pasta jar
Tracing or parchment paper
Scissors
String
Adhesive tape
Pen
Ruler
Flag patterns (page 76)
Black pen
Enough pasta to fill the jar
Opaque glass paint such as Ceramic à L'Eau in black, red, green, blue, and white
No 2 paintbrush
Hairdryer (optional)
Water
Domestic oven

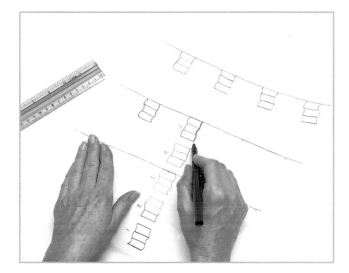

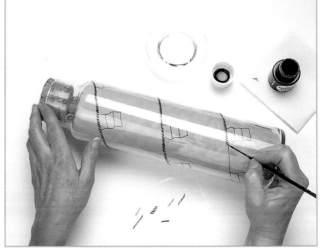

2 Remove the string and lay the paper flat. Place the flags equally on the line by measuring even gaps between them. Use the five variations of flags given and draw them along the line. You now have a pattern which will fit snugly into your pasta jar.

3 Place the pattern into the jar and fill it with pasta to hold it in place. Paint the line with the black paint using a straight line, or a rope pattern if you are more adventurous, but experiment first on a piece of cellophane. Use the hairdryer to speed the process if you are impatient.

4 Paint the green section on each flag next, again allowing the color to dry before moving on. If necessary, mix a little blue with the green to achieve the correct shade.

5 Change the water and clean your paintbrush very well before painting the white part of each flag. Allow it to dry and then finish with the red and leave for 24 hours to dry before baking, following the manufacturer's instructions.

TEXTURED FRUIT TUMBLERS

There is no need for a template when the design is embossed in the glass as it is in these tumblers. This makes it a good project for a beginner. The tumblers are made from recycled glass and similar glassware is widely available. Use the idea on embossed jugs and wine bottles too, and choose jewel-like colors to produce a luscious look.

1 Thoroughly wash and dry the glasses in hot soapy water to remove any trace of grease and then dry them in a cool oven. Choose the colors you want to use and test them on a sheet of cellophane before starting on the glassware. Start by painting the lemons and orange slices with the yellow paint.

YOU WILL NEED

| Embossed glasses |
| Porcelaine 150 glass paints in orange, pink, purple, yellow, and green |
| Cellophane |
| No 2 paintbrush |
| Water |
| Kitchen paper towels |
| Domestic oven |

TIP

You can easily unite a collection of mismatched textured glassware by painting it in the same colors.

2 Using the orange paint, highlight the citrus slices to give them depth and a rich, fruity look. You may wish to build up colors by using two or more coats of paint.

3 We have chosen a cerise pink for these cherries, but if you prefer a brighter look, use a strong red or even a really dark mix of purple and red paint to imitate juicy black cherries.

4 The grapes are painted using the purple. Do not worry if the paint does not lie flat on the surface of the grapes, as the nature of the paint is such that it has an uneven effect. In this project this is of benefit, as it reflects the natural bloom of the fruits.

5 Finally, paint the foliage green. Leave the tumblers to dry for 24 hours and then bake according to manufacturer's instructions. Wash the glasses before use.

RED GALLERY

Sundae glass

Below: The top part of the glass was sponged with red, while gold was used for the lower part. Once dry, tiny spots of gold outliner were added as a decorative pattern.

Fleur de lys jar

Bottom left: Flat-sided jelly jars are ideal for decorating. This one was sponged first and then the design added with gold outliner.

Triangular red bottle

Bottom: Sponging forms the basis of the pattern on both these bottles. Outliner has been used for the relief patterns.

Valentine platter

Simple and sweet for the one you love!

Faceted jar

This design was inspired by old glassware and could be used very effectively in a range of colors on a set of sundae glasses or tumblers.

Octagonal dish

Positive and negative stenciling has been used to decorate this dish with heart motifs.

Heart-shaped crown bottle

Bottom: Colored glass bottles are widely available and are easy to decorate. This one features simple but effective designs.

Bow glass

The bottom part of this glass was sponged with gold. Once dry, the bow motif was stencilled on. You could cut your own stencil or use a commercial one.

Strawberry cup

Bottom: You need some artistic skills to reproduce this design, but it could be simplified or even stenciled. Why not paint a set of glass cups with a selection of fruits, and use them for serving fruit teas?

Faceted pitcher

This wonderful old pitcher was found at a local thrift store. It lends itself to this kind of decoration. Similar pieces of glassware are easy to find. A combination of painting and relief work has been used.

Spotty bottle

Soda pop bottles come in a great range of shapes and sizes which are ideal for revamping and re-using.

CHRISTMAS PLATTER

It seems a pity to cover the design on this Christmas platter but it is perfect for serving up Christmas cookies on a wintry day. The pattern is on the back, making a series of these plates great to use as special dinner plates if they are washed with care. Christmas trees or ivy leaves could be substituted for holly.

1 Make the reverse stencil for the gold edging by folding a piece of paper in half and then into fourths. Fold in half diagonally twice so that you have 16 layers of paper with the fold lines radiating out from the central point. Use the ruler to measure the radius of the flat base of the platter, and then mark this measurement on the paper from the central point outward. Cut the "V" shape as shown in the photograph. Open out the paper (you should have a circle with a pointed edge) and lightly spray with aerosol mount. Leave for a few seconds and then stick to the back of the plate.

YOU WILL NEED

Glass plate — ours is 10 iinches in diameter
Ruler
Paper
Pen or pencil
Scissors
Scalpel with no 11 blade
Cutting mat
Holly leaf and star patterns (page 76)
Aerosol adhesive spray mount
Solvent-based glass paints in gold, red, and green (we mixed emerald and chartreuse for the holly)
Fine sponge or fur fabric
No 2 paintbrush

VARIATIONS

Why not make a complete set of Christmas glasses to match the plate? The holly design could be reduced on a photocopier and the holly and berries painted around the glass bowl. Sponge gold on the base, stem, and bottom of the bowl.

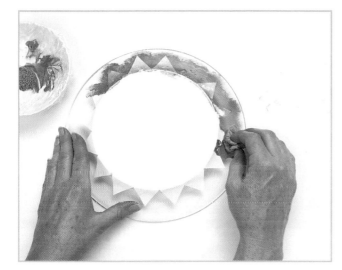

2 Pour a little of the gold paint into the saucer and then sponge it over the edge of the template all the way around. Apply the paint densely at the edge of the template to give a sharp outline and less densely near the rim of the plate. Remove the template and leave to dry.

3 Meanwhile, cut the holly stencils, using the holly patterns on page 76. As the points of the leaves are very fine, it is worth using a new scalpel blade before attempting to cut them. Cut out the stars too. Use a cutting mat to protect the worksurface and leave a border of about ½ inch around each one. Lightly spray the backs with the aerosol adhesive.

4 Stencil the gold stars in the center and allow them to dry. Mix the green paints to achieve the desired color, and then stencil about three leaves around the base of the plate, using the sponge. Use the photo as a guide and vary the angle of the leaves as you go. We have given you three different leaf sizes to make the design look more interesting. Use the cocktail stick to etch in the veining details of each leaf before stenciling the next three.

5 Use the paintbrush to fill in the gaps with the holly berries. We have mixed a rich ruby red color for them. Leave to dry thoroughly before using.

TEMPLATES

The templates shown here are actual size.
They may be easily enlarged or reduced on a
photocopier to suit the size of the glass to
be decorated.

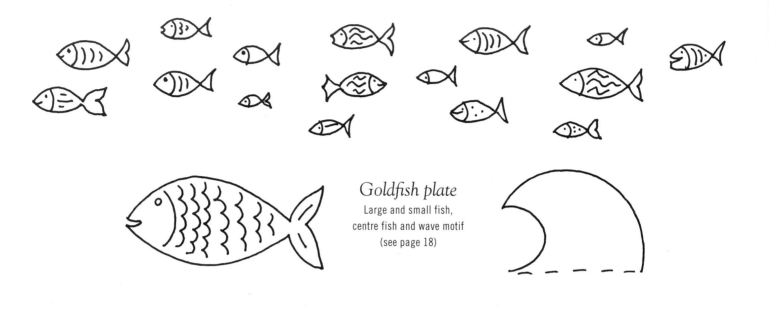

Goldfish plate
Large and small fish,
centre fish and wave motif
(see page 18)

Olive oil bottle
Olive spray (see page 20)

Ruby and gold sundae glasses
Leaf and tendril design (see page 28)

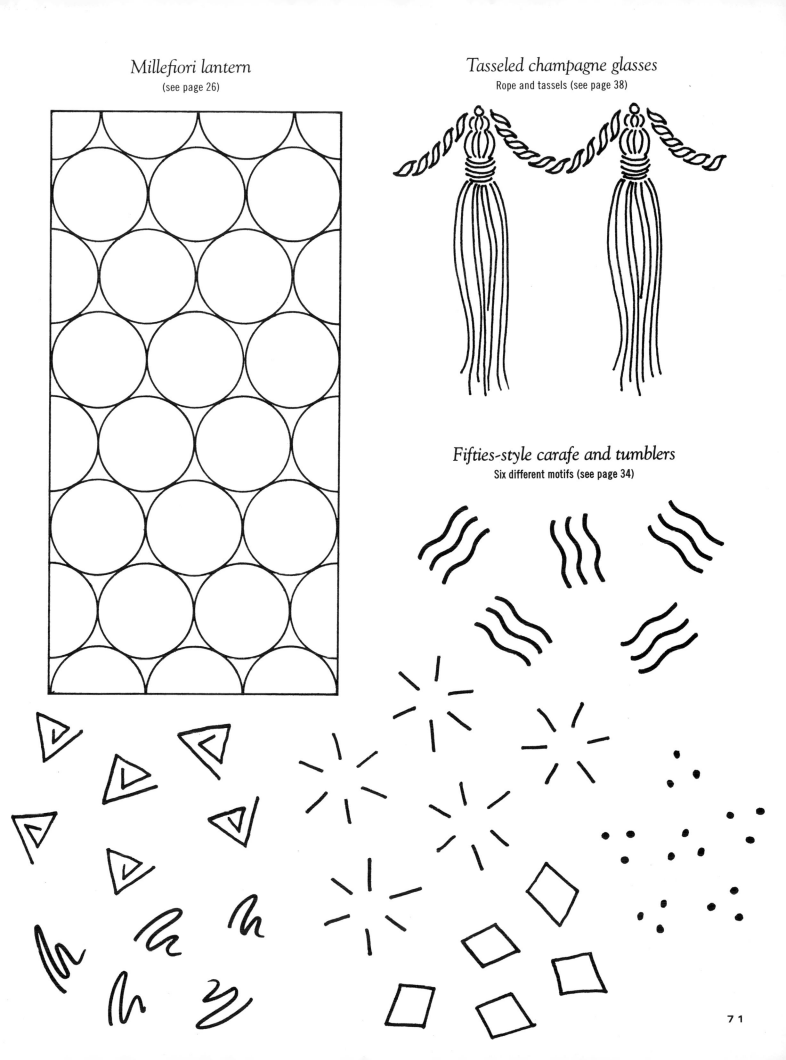

Millefiori lantern
(see page 26)

Tasseled champagne glasses
Rope and tassels (see page 38)

Fifties-style carafe and tumblers
Six different motifs (see page 34)

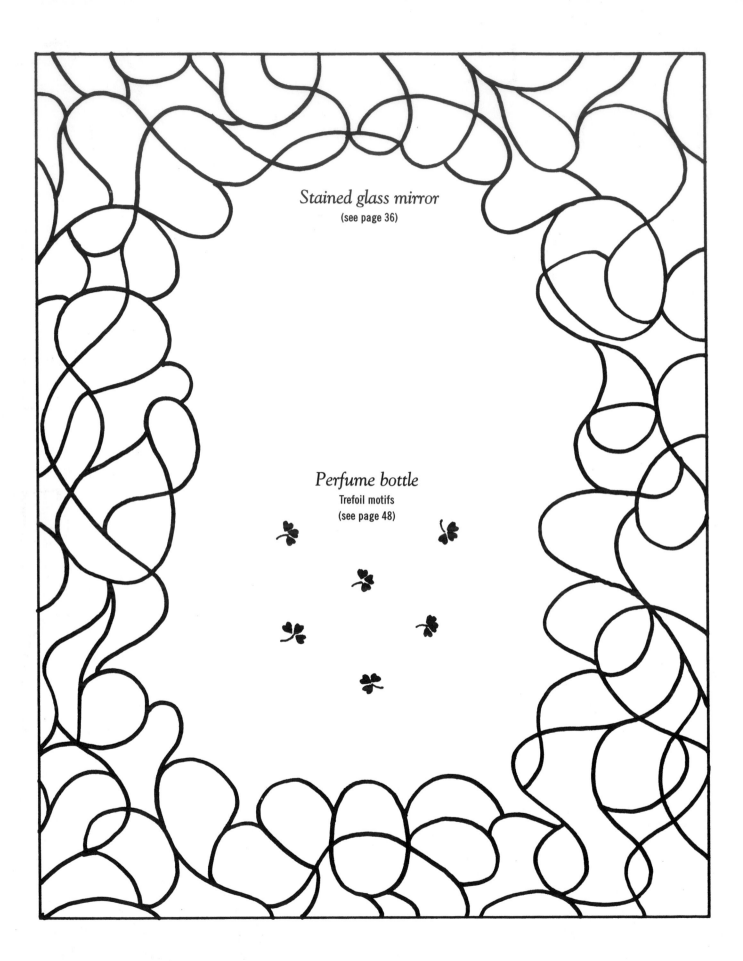

Stained glass mirror
(see page 36)

Perfume bottle
Trefoil motifs
(see page 48)

Frosted glass window
Rooster, heart, and blocks pattern
for stencil-making
(see page 52)

Starry oil burner
Star shapes (see page 44)

Floral roundels

(see page 54)

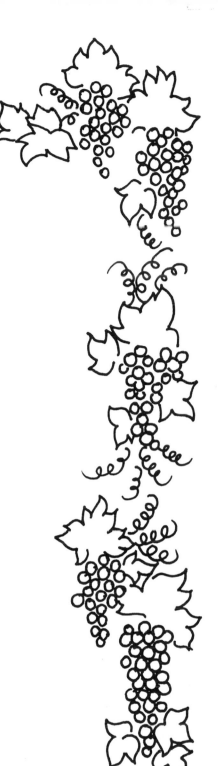

Grapevine clip frame

(see page 60)

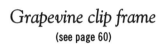

Pasta jar (see page 62)

Christmas platter (see page 68)

Practice patterns for getting started (see page 9)

Floral border
(Used on book cover – repeat
the design for each corner
using both sides of the tracing)

Getting started heart stencil design
(see page 12)

ACKNOWLEDGEMENTS

The authors and publishers would like to say a
very big thank you to Pébéo, in particular John
Wright of Pébéo UK and Carol Hook from Clear
Communications Ltd, who have been so generous
in their supply of paints, especially Porcelaine
150 and Vitrail, which we have used almost
exclusively in this book.

Thank you to Clearcraft for their beautiful glass
oil burners and to the Egyptian House who
generously supplied us with a selection of their
lovely colored and recycled glass. Thanks to
Shona for her patience, stamina, and superb
photographs and to Yvonne for letting us write
this book! Thank you to the Cambridge branch of
Emmaus, the self-help group for the homeless, for
having such an abundance of glassware at
incredibly good prices just crying out to be
painted (we hope you can also buy your glassware
from an equally good cause.)

For further information about Pébéo products
please contact Pébéo at the following address:

In the U.S.:
Pebeo of America, Inc.
Airport Road, P.O. Box 717
Swanton, VT 05488
Tel: 8192-829-5012
Fax: 819-821-4151
e-mail: pebeo@multim-medias.ca
Internet: www.pebeo.com

In Canada:
Pebeo Canada
1905 Roy St.
Sherbrooke, QC J1H 3L9
Tel: 8192-829-5012
Fax: 819-821-4151
e-mail: pebeo@multim-medias.ca
Internet: www.pebeo.com

INDEX

adhesive putty 44
adhesive stenciling film 11
Antiqued Etruscan-style vase 32-33

Black, silver, and gold gallery 46-47
Blue, silver, and gold gallery 40-41
bottles
    olive oil 20
    perfume 48
brushes 8, 10

cellophane 8, 9
Christmas platter 68-69
cleaning glassware 9
clip frame 69
cockerel motif 52
cocktail sticks 8, 11, 13
cotton buds 8, 10
craft knife 8, 11
cutting stencils 11

Decorated wine glasses 50-51
denture cleaner 8

East European glassware 15
embellishments 14
equipment 8
etching 13, 21, 53, 61, 69

Faux tortoiseshell plate 22-23
feathering 27
Fifties-style carafe and tumblers 34-35
fish motif 18
flag motif 62
Floral roundels 54-55
florist's wire 8, 20
food safety 9, 14
frame 60
Frosted glass window 52-53
fur fabric 10, 52, 60, 68

galleries 24-25, 30-31, 40-41, 46-47, 56-57, 66-67
gel paint 9
glass nuggets 9, 14
glass painting products 9
glasses
    champagne 38

decorated wine glasses 50
    textured fruit tumblers 64
Goldfish plate 18-19
graduated color 10
Grapevine clip frame 60-61

hairdryer 8, 22, 37, 44, 62
hand rest 21
Historical gallery 30-31

inspiration for designs 15

jelly jar 8, 9

knitting needles 13

lantern 26
leaf motif 20, 29

Marbled plate 58-59
marbling 13, 22, 58
masking 12
masking tape 12
materials 8
matt medium 9, 33, 44
metalic effect 32
Millefiori lantern 26-27
mirror 36
motifs
    Christmas 68
    cockerel 52
    fifties'-style 34
    fish 18
    flag 62
    flowers 54
    grapes 60
    hearts 52
    holly 68
    leaves 28, 60, 68
    olives 20
    Shaker 12
    stars 44, 68
    tassels 38
    tendrils 29
    trefoils 48

nail polish remover 8
narrow necked bottles 14, 20

oil burner 44
Olive oil bottles 20-21
opaque paint 62

outlining 9-10
oven-bake outliners 26, 34
oven-bake paints 9, 18, 42, 48, 50, 64

paint, types of 9
Pasta jar 62-63
Perfume bottle 48-49
pipettes 22, 23, 58
plates
    Christmas 68
    faux tortoiseshell 22
    goldfish 18
    marbled 58
    snowflake 13
    sunflower 42
polyurethane varnish 23
practice templates 9

Red gallery 66-67
relief pattern 12
reverse painting 14
reverse stenciling 12
rhinestones 37
roundels 54
rubber bands 28, 50
Ruby and gold sundae glasses 28-29

safety 8, 9
scalpel 8, 11
sequins 37
snowflake plate 13
solvent-based paint 9, 13, 18, 20, 22, 28, 36, 54, 58, 60, 68
sourcing glassware 8
sponge dishcloths 10
sponge dot applicators 11
sponging 10, 18, 32, 48, 51, 61, 69
stained glass 9
Stained glass mirror 36-37
Starry oil burner 44-45
stenciling 11-12, 52
sundae glasses 28

Tasseled champagne glasses 38-39
tea glasses 28
techniques
    etching 13, 21, 53, 61, 69

marbling 13, 22, 58
sponging 10, 18, 32, 48, 51, 61, 69
stenciling 11-12, 52
templates 70-77
Textured fruit tumblers 64-65
tortoiseshell 22
transferring designs 14
Turquoise gallery 56-57
typist's eraser 13

vase 32
Venetian glassware 15, 30

wallpaper paste 13, 58
water-based gel paints 9
water-based paints 9
window panel 52

Yellow gallery 24-25

Related Titles from Lark Books

Creative Glass Techniques
Fusing • Painting • Lampwork
By Bettina Eberle

$24.95 Paperback ($34.95 Can.),
152 pages, 160 color photos

ISBN 1-887374-30-2

Distributed by Random House

Making Glass Beads
By Cindy Jenkins

$21.95 Hardback ($29.95 Can.),
112 pages, 250 color photos

ISBN 1-887374-16-7

Distributed by Random House